In Your Garden

Lindsey Simms

BookLeaf Publishing

Presentation by *BookLeaf Publishing*

Web: www.bookleafpub.com

E-mail: info@bookleafpub.com

ISBN: 9789357745826

First edition 2023

DEDICATION

To my grandmother, Lavonne Adams. For you I'd do absolutely anything - even become a poet.

PREFACE

All of these poems are crafted from real
memories between me and my grandmother,
who was my best friend growing up. As I went
off to college, her dementia grew worse and our
relationship deteriorated due to her health.

We've missed out on so much together, including
many milestones - high school and college
graduations, recitals, my engagement, and
recently my wedding. Things we talked about all
the time when I was growing up flew by while
she sat at home suffering in silence.

People don't talk enough about how much it
hurts to lose someone who's still alive, to mourn
a relationship that will never be the same.

I hope this book helps those in similar situations,
because God knows I needed this when I was in
the midst of losing my best friend.

My Grandma

My grandma smells of fresh soil and peonies,
of warm tea and crayon dust.
Tootsie rolls and belly laughs
you give freely
when I am three,
but soon I grow smart
and find where you keep them hidden
on the counter in the kitchen.

Bright colors glisten across the walls
when sunlight pours in
at just the right angle;
my paintings from school on full display -
two crude hearts, a square,
dilapidated triangles.

Art class is my favorite place to be,
but my favorite place where we go
just you and I
is where the flowers grow.

In Your Garden

You suggest we start a secret club
over gingersnaps and sweet tea
as we sit in your garden
trimming and weeding,
and I laugh and nod because I am six
and in love with the warmth I feel
in my belly every time I
make you smile by plucking petals and
scattering them at my feet.
Anything to make you happy.

Secret Club

Mama and Daddy bring me over to visit
every weekend, but it's not enough.
We live close by, just up the street -
I feel tall when I peer out the window and see
your sunflowers lean against
the garage wall's dark brick.
"Grandma is busy," Mommy lifts and
plops me back onto the couch.
I huff and cross my arms.
Mommy just doesn't know
about our secret club.

Metropolis

I often try to count
how many birdhouses you've collected
and stuffed into every
nook and cranny
in your house and garden,
but I always lose count and
have to start over again.
They sprout and spread like the ivy
that sneaks along your house.

I spot the white one I found
at a yard sale for you -
$5 was worth it to see your smile
as you hung it proudly in the
center of your yard.
But still I wonder why birds
even need houses anyways.
"What's the purpose of
collecting all this?"

You laugh,
hands on hips as you
survey the metropolis
you've constructed.
"Because they bring me joy."

Inspired by your answer,
I begin to collect what brings me joy -
Words
phrases
and ideas.
My yard sales are my books,
articles, overheard conversations.
I gather my harvest,
scrawl them on bits of scrap paper
and shove them in desk drawers
behind shelves and stuffed binders.

I pull them out
every once in a while
to marvel at and count
but I always
lose track
and have to
begin again.

Tending to My Garden

My collection cannot be displayed
or hung on branches in a garden -
which is a pity because my
internal private collection
deserves recognition -
these words and ideas
stories of things in my head
should be seen, heard,
felt, read.

My wrists will sometimes shake,
quaking from the words inside me
trying to escape,
buzzing like the bees in your garden.
"write write write"
they bumble as they
bounce from flower to flower.

I scribble sentences of words I collect,
the phrases and stories
starting to spill,
and after picking and planting,
building and trimming,
my hands will be
finally quiet and still.

I wish I could hang these
words off of trees.

Nostalgia

I spend every Saturday
in the garden with you
cutting roses with craft scissors
and watching snails soak
in your birdbath.
You show me how
ants open peony buds
and how to harvest red tongues
to taste when walking in the woods.

Together we explore
every acre of Flood City -
Inclined Plane rides and penny candy,
taking the trolley
downtown to the library,
collecting fern fossils in the valley
and blueberries in the hills.

Summers are spent barefoot
catching crawfish and
speckled salamanders
in Stackhouse Park.
Husking corn on the porch swing,
and reading in the garden until
fireflies chase us home after dark.

Bicycles thrown on garden grass
because everyone knows your
cookies are the best
in the neighborhood,
but maybe I'm just biased.

Aging Gracefully

Aging gracefully is
waking up early
just because watering your
flowerbeds is your
absolute favorite thing to do
on a Saturday morning,

and you chat with Kitty,
your neighbor and friend,
who brings over spare rhubarb
since her plant grew too
much and she wanted to share
because she remembers how much
you loved her rhubarb pie last summer.

It's taking your grandkids to yard sales
and teaching them everything you know,
reading your Bible with only the
squeak of the rusted
porch swing spring
to keep you company
in the late evening.

It's collecting puzzles and paintings
because it makes you happy,

and you see a glimmer of yourself
in each piece you pick.
It's knowing your garden will
live again come spring
so you don't mourn the passing
flowers that die,
but instead just grab
your shawl and tea
when the leaves change.

It's a cracked window,
crickets before bed
with a side of spinning vinyl.

It's keeping pictures by your bedside
as the memories become fuzzy,
hoping that having them close
will keep them from fading entirely.

It's digging
planting
and uprooting,
and starting over again
each morning.

Little Nowhere Town

Johnstown is your home -
the PA hills your playground,
each farmhouse a memory
as we drive by in your car.

Past, present, and future you
can all be found within
this rust belt town;
your roots run deep
and are covered in
local coal dust.

But you want me to leave.
"On to bigger and better things,"
your voice lilts, like a
hopeful song
that turns sour
in my preteen ears.

These hills are big enough
to be my home too.

Thrift Store Wisdom

"There are three things you don't want
secondhand,"
you comment as we weave through
our favorite flea market.

"Lingerie, makeup, and men."
I set the lipstick back on the shelf
for somebody else
without a grandma to find.

Too Busy

To me you are eternal
never changing in pattern or design
as all grandmas should be.

You are aged yet ageless,
timed in stature
yet timeless in step
as you prance through the garden
weeding and clipping,
brown hair tucked back.

My safe space,
tucked in your garden and
always available
when I need you.
But when your design
starts changing
shifting
cracking
the familiar gets confusing and
words get more jumbled,
and the weeds get too thick
to be conquered
by your weathered wrists,
I am busy.

Busy with college essays and
senior ceremonies, summer flings and
saying goodbye to my life before
turning eighteen -

And so there you stay
tucked in my back pocket -
the garden a haze of nostalgia,
comforting me into thinking you're fine
because I'm too busy
already pulling away
to check in.

The Beginning of the End

It was a family affair,
but you weren't there
to wave me off to school
one last time as I
packed up my things
and drove off to campus.

You promised you'd help me pack
but instead you were in bed
and not feeling well again,
anxious thoughts keeping you
from stepping outside.

Boxes I saved filled with notes and
birthday cards and
trinkets from you
I place carefully on my bed.

Some kids get hugs or kisses
or pictures of moments,
but I have things to
serve as my snapshots
of time gone by -
time capsules
for my memories.

A vintage pin, a thrifted vase -
my dorm is a place
I realize you'll
most likely never visit.
A place where I'll exist
without you in it.
Is such a thing even possible?

I put the vase filled with
flowers from your garden
on my desk.
I guess this is something
we'll both have to navigate.

The Fruits of Your Labor

Knowledge really is like oxygen -
I take big gulps
every day in class
like I'm drowning, yet I'm
more alive than I ever was
in that dusty old town.
My wordy scribbles
become more defined
and sharp with practice.
I can't wait to show
you my writing -
that one paper
and that essay
I stayed up
all night to tweak
until just right.
That one story I wrote
and screenplay I'm still writing.
Something I can thrust in your hands
when I'm away at college,
so you can still have me close.
You're the reason I'm here
that I made it out,
so now I need
evidence that your time
wasn't wasted
on me.

Bittersweet Victories

You were supposed to be
at my spring recital,
the Christmas concert,
my senior year musical -
I reserved the front row
just for you
because you invested
so much in
my music lessons and
passions for the arts
that surely you'd want
to take part
in every victory,
every recital, blue ribbon,
casting call and show.
It would be easier if the excuses
were more black and white,
but this gray area is
getting hard to navigate.
If only I'd done these things sooner
or invested more time,
then we could enjoy
these moments together
Or
How dare they hug their grandma

right in front of me.
They know my story.
How's it fair his grandma is here
when mine
who's worked so hard
to get me here
isn't here
and will never
be here?
It's selfish and pointless,
but I feel it anyway.
Like a half-healed wound,
rubbed raw with
every win.

Priorities

"Come home," the voice cracks.
It's 4 am.
Highlighted notes from
Screenwriting and Global Lit
swim across my eyes
as I brush the study guides
off my face.
4 hours until my first final.
I grimace into the receiver.
"Come again?"
Grandma.
Icy steps.
Broken arm.
Grandma
I forget to lock the door
behind me in my haste.
Finals be damned.

Get Well Soon

The room is cold
and man-made and dark,
like a tomb.
Let her out
I want to shout
at the nurses passing by.
How can she heal in a place without the sun?
I open the blinds
and sunbeams fall onto her bed
as dust dances in the air.

You lie there asleep,
your skin as cold
as the steps you slipped on
just last week,
and I wish I could take you
to your garden
and let the fresh soil seep
back into your skin.
Sunbeams will color your face
and heal your cracked arm.

But I settle for bringing
some of your garden to you.
The bouquet may be store-bought but
roses have always been your favorite.

Fragments

My grandma smells of dust and salty
tears, of burnt coffee and fog.
I sift through years
of memories when I
come to visit,

every time hopeful that if I
point out the right thing
you'll remember that time
at that one place
three years ago when we
scored that gorgeous
birdhouse shaped like a church
that hangs atop your lilac bush.
Or those cute red earrings,
your favorite color,
just last fall.

That wind chime,
from that one time
on Luzerne Street we stopped
at a yard sale and bought
three dish sets
for my future place
because you know how much
I love cookware.

But instead of unlocking anything,
you smile and mutter how
you've managed to burn
the coffee again.

An Internal Struggle

"C'mon Grandma, let's go outside."
But the rain-
"is lovely in the spring! Let's grab your-"
and my shoes
"will be fine. Let's pick some flowers."
There's mud.
"Or you can sit on the
porch swing
and listen to the rain,
your favorite sound."
No, I don't think that's a good idea.
"Fresh air will help."
It won't.
"Come on, you love your garden-"
Not today.
"and being outside-"
I can't
"But the-"
I can't
"Please, just-"
I can't

I can't

I can't

I slam my car door as I leave.
No, *I* can't.

Club Membership Pending

Garden parties with
thrifted China, and
strawberry milk
as a late-night treat
while the record spins
in the sunroom.
Falling leaves and
pool splashes;
movie nights with
puzzles and reading glasses.
Newspaper clippings
of weekend rummage sales,
painting birdhouses and
salty peanut shells.
Setting the table with
fresh-picked flowers,
guitar lessons and
porch swing prayers -

Everything I miss
about us
and our secret club,
our grandma-grandkid
best friendship,
drips off you

like morning dew
every day.
The haze that holds you captive
is my greatest adversary.

New Routine

Things aren't easier,
but they are good.

I show you pictures
of my wedding,
new husband holding a starfish
on our honeymoon,
me in my dress by the water.
Work trips and new pets
and our current tiny house,
garden-less.

I paint your nails
while you hum,
sometimes you squeeze my hand
extra tight and
I think you break through the fog
and remember me,
and I hope you're happy,
with or without
our memories.

Ethereal

Ashes to ashes
and dust to dust.
Blessed is our endurance,
yet fragility is what
makes us the most
human.

www.ingramcontent.com/pod-product-compliance
Lightning Source LLC
Chambersburg PA
CBHW050750180726
48003CB00020B/2318